T0065480

REBIRTH
THROUGH
RADIATION

LOLITA SCOTT

authorHOUSE

AuthorHouse™
1663 Liberty Drive
Bloomington, IN 47403
www.authorhouse.com
Phone: 833-262-8899

Published by AuthorHouse 03/05/2021

ISBN: 978-1-6655-1923-6 (sc)
ISBN: 978-1-6655-1924-3 (e)

Print information available on the last page.

Scripture quotations marked KJV are from the Holy Bible, King James Version (Authorized Version). First published in 1611. Quoted from the KJV Classic Reference Bible, Copyright © 1983 by The Zondervan Corporation.

This book is printed on acid-free paper.

And in the dungeon there was no water, but mire; so Jeremiah sank in the mire.

—Jeremiah 36:8 KJV

I'm remembering these family members who proceeded me in death: my father, Ellis Hinton; my mother, "Sweet Pea" (Willie Dean); and my two older brothers, Ellis Hinton Jr. and Bobby Hinton. I'm also reflecting on other victims of cancer, both alive and deceased. We've all fought a good fight!

CONTENTS

ACKNOWLEDGMENTS

I would like to thank and publicly honor my husband, Bruce Scott, for his faithfulness to our marriage vows. He loves me in sickness and in health.

I'm very grateful for my siblings, who were very supportive during my affliction. I commend my son, "Lil Bruce," for giving me his valuable time and thoughts. Finally, I must thank my spiritual covering, Pastor Pitts, First Lady, and Elder Campbell. Their prayers moved mountains!

INTRODUCTION

I would like to open this book by defining the word *dungeon*, seeing that it's not a word used in our everyday language. A dungeon is an underground place of darkness with intentional isolation. We are typically sent there for disciplinary action.

That is where my diagnosis of cancer led me emotionally. The dungeon wasn't totally foreign to me. I'd stepped into this dungeon a few times before. I'd gone here when experiencing the grief of six miscarriages, which included a set of twins, and the death of my mother (because I was the youngest of eight, my mother and I were very dear to each other). My mother's death had somewhat equipped me for the death of my youngest brother; we were close, and I admired him a great deal as well.

Even with all these dreadful incidents, I'd never experienced the dungeon in its entirety. I'd always managed to allow the door of the dungeon to remain open so the light would lead me upward. That light I speak of is Jesus. However, in the season of sadness of my cancer diagnosis, I was angry at my Savior. In fact, I slammed the door on Him. How much grief did my Lord expect me to take on? I thought I had fought very hard not to lose my mind when I suffered the miscarriage of my twins and the death of my mother.

Yet in all that adversity, the Lord did allow me to have my magnificent husband and adorable son, Bruce and Little Bruce. Previously, I had always heard one of their voices when I was in my dungeon of depression, which would lead me out. However, that wasn't the case this time. As hours passed throughout the day, I would retreat deeper and deeper into my own personal dungeon. I did not want to be led out.

Everyone seemed to have words of comfort. They meant well, but honestly, I wished they all would shut up and go home. Oh, I just wanted to go into my dark dungeon and cry. I didn't want to fight. I was tired of fighting. Couldn't I just enjoy the rest of my life on earth? How grateful I am that God was not offended by my temper tantrums. Neither was my husband, Bruce.

Now that I have shared with you my place of shelter during the diagnosis, allow me to share the journey of the diagnosis itself.

At the time, life was full of glorious possibilities. I was very secure as an entrepreneur. My child development center was flourishing. I was on the brink of establishing another one. My family life and marriage were great. In spite of the sicknesses and deaths mentioned earlier, I managed to master life's storms. Never, never could I have imagined such a devastating storm as cancer would bombard my life.

God was faithful, allowing the Holy Spirit to bring scripture to my memory, such as this one: "Whoever hears my word and does it, his house is built on the rock. Though the storms and winds blow, it won't destroy the house" (Matthew 7:24). That was gonna be my hope. The gates of Hell would not prevail, even though I was walking past them daily during my ordeal. God walked right beside me, whispering He would never leave me nor forsake me. Yet that whisper wasn't loud enough. The voice inside my head, which I now know was the enemy, screamed louder. It was the accuser of the brethren (Revelation 12:9–11) making me feel ashamed by suggesting I wasn't spiritual enough—in fact, making me believe I wasn't saved at all.

Throughout this book, I will emphasize the love that God has for His people. Hold on to that truth.

It is vital your faith worketh by love (Galatians 5:6). He who freely gave His son, won't He give us all things? (Romans 8:32). Surely, this includes healing. After all, by His stripes, we are healed. Yet, that was the first lie that the enemy spoke in my ear: "God doesn't love you." Readers, please never let the devil allow you to doubt God's love.

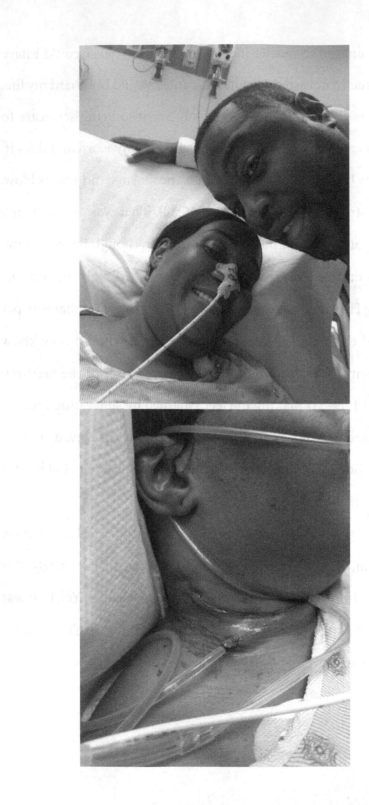

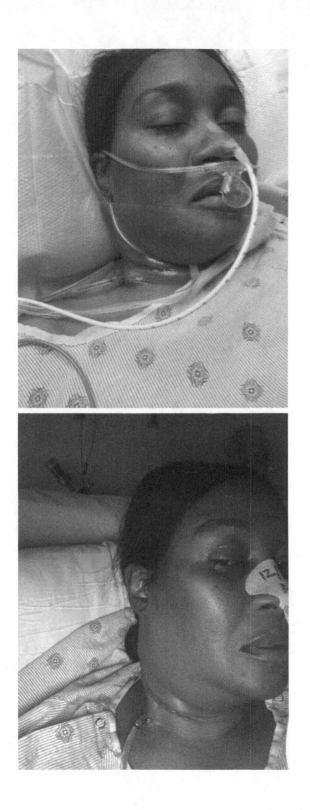

CHAPTER 1

DUNGEON OF DIAGNOSIS

And in the dungeon there was no water, but mire; so

Jeremiah sank in the mire.

—Jeremiah 36:8 KJV

A dungeon is an underground place filled with darkness, and it serves the purpose of punishment. It creates feelings of isolation and intimidation.

My diagnosis made me feel exactly like a prisoner. I thought I was being punished. Therefore, I sat in the darkness of my mind, which became my dungeon. This dungeon was not foreign to me. You see, I had visited this place several times before, such as while grieving the death of my father; I would refer to those times as taking me into the dungeon of depression. My parents had me late in life. I was their little prize—at least I thought so. Being the youngest of eight children had many perks as well as pitfalls. In any event, we were a close-knit family. To have the head member of that family permanently removed was horrid. My father always made me feel so special. Then, to watch my mother maneuver without him was unbearable.

I suffered in the dungeon of depression during this time of grieving. I suffered from "would've, could've, should've" syndrome, as many do during the bereavement of a loved one. You see, I blamed myself because at the time, I was a nursing student, and I felt as if I could have resuscitated my father. For a long time, I felt I might have caused his death. However, that was a lie told to me in the dungeon of my mind. My father had expired before I even began CPR. Nevertheless, the dungeon held me captive to this guilt for quite a while.

Life in the dungeon is intensely dark. Lies are spoken in this dungeon; it's simply indescribable. Fortunately for me, at the time, I was in a courtship with a wonderful man, Bruce Scott, who has now been my husband for almost thirty years. Our courtship was quite wholesome. We were always together. The company of Bruce brought light to my darkness and depression.

There were times when Bruce and I shared a place together in the dungeon. The times when I had six miscarriages, which included a set of twins, were of great suffering for both of us. We agreed that this was too traumatic, so we gave up trying. We simply just raised our only son, Little Bruce, who has given us much joy.

Even then, I felt I was being punished. For what, I didn't quite know. So many unfit mothers were having children. Yet I wasn't able to carry to term. Why was that? I asked myself in the dungeon. I never received an answer. Nothing but lies are given to you in the dungeon of darkness.

Seven years after the death of my father, my mother passed. I had always told my mother that when they lowered her into the ground, I was going to jump in with her. Even though I didn't jump in physically, I did jump into a dark hole emotionally. For ten years, in the privacy of my bedroom, I cried every night. Could all these experiences combined have created enough toxicity to cause cancer? I don't know, but they gave me a lengthy visitation by doom.

Let's take a break from the dungeon. I would now like to reflect on my diagnosis. At the time, outside of the death of my two brothers, life had been grand. I had learned to cope with the loss of my family members. I was now an entrepreneur, having ownership of a day care center located on the South Side of Chicago. And I was on the brink of opening another. I felt very accomplished.

My marriage had survived all of life's ups and downs. I was living life interrupted. I attributed that to my spiritual health. Bruce was definitely the priest of our home, as well as an ordained elder. I thought I was safe from any further storms. However, life has seasons, and seasons have storms. It is written that man born of a woman has few days and is much trouble (Job 14:1).

So I was in a good place until one evening, while out having dinner with Bruce, I felt some discomfort. I was having difficulty swallowing. Bruce and I weren't too alarmed. We simply agreed that it would be addressed in my upcoming physical.

During my physical, the physician's assistant noticed something, yet she didn't seem concerned. However, as a lump began to grow, Bruce urged me to see his primary doctor.

The days of walk-in appointments were over. I had to wait over a week as the lump continued to grow. While examining me, the physician, Dr. Lawson, was puzzled by the lump. To rule out any malignancies, he referred me to an ear, nose, and throat specialist. For this appointment, I also had to wait—two weeks of waiting for a specialist while dark thoughts of cancer invaded my mind.

I was not aware that it would be, but the biopsy was truly horrid. I don't believe it had to be, but the doctor's bedside manner was diabolical! Because I was unaware of this, I had allowed Bruce to sit outside. Without informing me of the logistics of the procedure, the doctor jabbed a three-inch needle—I mean literally—into my neck. I messaged Bruce by text to come accompany me. The doctor continued the procedure without any compassion. I cried like a baby while Bruce comforted me.

On our ride home, the dungeon put forth its tentacles, suctioning me down into despair. I was a willing prisoner. I wasn't interested in any of Bruce's "sermons on the mount." I was sore from the biopsy and anxious about the outcome.

The seven-day wait for the results seemed like an eternity. Bruce prayed over me daily as I watched my neck increase in size. I had nowhere to resort to except the dungeon of my mind. While there in the dungeon, all I could visualize were others who had fallen prey to cancer. Those who had lost the battle continually came up before my eyes. I wanted to escape this dungeon, but my thoughts held me captive. How was I to escape these thoughts? "For as he thinketh in his heart, so is he" (Proverbs 23:7 KJV).

That is when I began to get a grip and renew my mind. I commanded Satan to lose his hold on me by the authority I had in Jesus Christ. I would never visit that dark place again—or so I thought.

The morning that we were to discuss the results of my biopsy was gloomy. That did not help my morale. It was a typical autumn day in Chicago. The wind was strong and nearly blew me down. I held on to my strong husband. He smiled and whispered that no matter the outcome, we'd come out of it together. With these words, I felt as if I could walk on water (Matthew 14:30).

5

The doctor was a bit more behaved that day. This made me suspicious. He used medical terminology, seemingly stalling. Finally, I insisted he tell me if I had cancer, as if my insistence would deter my diagnosis. It didn't. I was diagnosed with stage three throat and neck cancer! Bruce began to coach me with his eyes not to break down. I didn't want to disappoint him, so I complied.

Riding home, I was screaming in silence. I had no choice but to take refuge in the dungeon. Strange as it was, I was not able to make entry into the dark place of my mind. I think it was because Bruce was quoting scripture. I resented him for his spiritual maturity.

My soul was invaded with emotions and questions. *Why am I suffering this affliction? I've never drank or smoked. Haven't I had my share of misery with six miscarriages?* I thought. *Why do I have to continually feel such anguish?* Immediately, scripture came to mind: Do we only receive the good from the hand of the Lord? (Job 2:10).

Because I have a close-knit family, they were waiting on my verdict. I told them the verdict was yes, I had cancer. I felt as if I had received a death sentence (Psalm 102:20). I contacted my middle sister, Corine, first. We both were quite emotional. Then, I shared with the others. In an ironic way, I felt pity for my siblings. After all, we had lost two brothers within five years to the same disease.

We waited ten days to discuss what method we would take to eradicate the cancer. In my time away, thoughts of death taunted me.

On the day of my prognosis, I felt inspired. I believe this was because of all the prayers that were made on my behalf. But when I saw that the patients on the floor all seemed as if they were on leave from the dungeon of diagnosis, my inspiration was arrested. Just as quickly as it was arrested, it was relinquished.

How could I be so tormented by a six-letter word—*cancer*—when there is a five-letter word that is above every other word—*Jesus*? With that thought, I lifted my head, for surely He is the lifter of my head (Psalm 3:3). And I made my way to my consultation.

The consultation was helpful; I gained informative options on how to rid me of this awful disease. I received sufficient time to discuss these with my husband. However, well-meaning people also shared their thoughts with me, and some ridiculed me for considering any type of medical intervention. They suggested that I trust God for supernatural healing.

My philosophy is "To my own self be true." Scripture also says according to faith, be it unto you (Matthew 9:29). My faith had not reached that measure. In my opinion, neither had the well-meaning people's. And I was not going to risk my life on other people's alleged faith! I acknowledged God, and He directed my path.

I struggled with not leaning on my own understanding. Ultimately, Bruce and I concluded that I would take the option of surgery with radiation following.

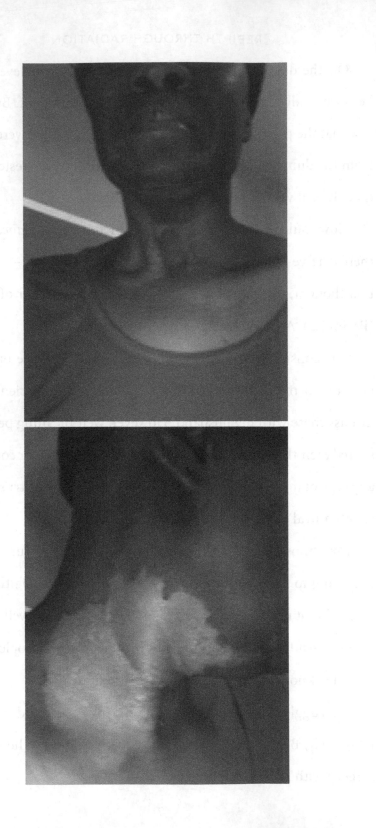

CHAPTER 2

DIVINITY DEFEATS DARKNESS

And the light shineth in the darkness and the darkness
comprehended it not.

—John 1:5 KJV

The Christmas holidays were swiftly approaching when Bruce brought
to my attention I hadn't planned the day care's annual Christmas
program. Planning the day care's annual Christmas program was
typically so exciting. How had I let this get past me? That is when
Bruce insisted that I inform the children's parents and my staff of my
health condition. Inwardly, I protested. I was in no hurry to make this
fact public. I didn't want my public to know of my affliction. I was

in a hard place. I wanted neither to be patronized nor to be pitied. What I desired was to be left to myself. Yet I knew that wasn't healthy.

During that time, the Christian cliché, "God knows how much you can bear," became so annoying to me. Even though this idea is true, it's not in scripture. Scripture does say, "There's nothing coming unto man that God has made a way of escape" (1 Corinthians 10:13). That made a difference. The scripture informed me that there is a way out when God says, "Okay, she can't bear any more."

My first discovery during this trial was I had to keep a pure heart. I couldn't become offended by what people said or didn't say. That would surely interrupt my healing. People meant well; they were just misinformed. I also discovered how I put pressure on myself. I felt unqualified for this battle. Later, I discovered all I had to do was believe. I had no power to heal myself. That was God's job. He had already performed that on Calvary. By His stripes, I was healed. I was healed before I got sick; I just needed to walk it out.

I had to fight the good fight of faith. To keep this mindset, I had to study God's Word. The devil made me feel quite guilty, telling me that if I hadn't been diagnosed, I wouldn't be reading the Bible. *Perhaps that is true; nevertheless, I am reading it,* I thought. *Therefore, you cannot continue to tell me untruths, such as I am not spiritual enough.*

I would cry out to God, asking Him, "Am I getting what I deserve?" That idea was simply a lie, I discovered. Satan was the accuser of the brethren (Revelation 12:10).

Still, I had questions for God. By the way, that was another untruth I had been taught: that we are not supposed to question God. If that were the case, why would He tell us, "If any man likes wisdom, let him ask God"? I needed to hear from God Himself. He was my only home during this time of adversity. The closest thing to His voice was His Word. So instead of going to the dungeon of my mind, I studied God's Word. I began with James 4:8, stating, "Draw nigh to God and He will draw nigh to you." This was going to be a long haul. December 16 was my surgery—after that, radiation. I prayed, "I believe, but help my unbelief. You promised never to leave me nor forsake me."

In between times of studying God's Word, life continued. I was still there to oversee the day care staff and children. I was so ill, but I saw myself happy. Praise is a powerful tool in times of helplessness. But your praise is tried. Oh, voices questioned me, asking whether my praise would be the same whether I were sick or well, rich or poor. My response was "I praise God for His mercy and His love toward me. God doesn't change, neither do my reasons for praising Him." I had plenty to praise God for, things like a good movie or a phone call from a longtime friend. It's the simple things in life that you learn to praise Him for. I praised Him for the times that I could enjoy. I praised Him for the one child I did have; I did not grumble about the six children I had lost.

However, the time of praise was interrupted by a phone call from my insurance company's billing department informing me of their inability to approve payment for my surgery. I explained to the representative that my surgery was scheduled for in a few days. She showed no remorse nor sensitivity.

I immediately fell to the floor and cried out to God, "Oh Lord, now what am I to do?" Just then, in the other room, I heard the song "Stand" playing: "What do you do when you've done all you can? You just stand!"

Was that my answer? If so, what could I stand on? I stood on God's Word. Before I knew it, I was singing old hymns, like "Hold to God's Unchanging Hand."

The joy of the Lord became my strength (Nehemiah 8:10).

First thing the next morning, I received a phone call from my insurance company's billing department saying they had approved my surgery after all. I can explain what happened. I do believe that the original call was an attempt to put me in a state of fear. Fear weakens one's faith, and praise is the highest form of faith.

The night before my surgery, I could not sleep. But I knew I had a long day ahead and I needed to rest. I remembered someone had told me, "If you ever have trouble sleeping, read your Bible." So that's exactly what I did. I came across the scripture, "He gives His beloved sleep" (Psalm 127:2).

The next day, we arrived at the hospital one hour before the scheduled time. My family was there to meet me. I felt so very proud of them for standing at attention. That is how we had been raised—*all for one, and one for all; united we stand, and divided we fall.* The enemy loves to divide and conquer. He seeks to keep you offended by small matters. If offended, you will withdraw and become isolated from loved ones. I'm not saying we are the perfect family. But we have learned to put our differences aside during hard times.

My pastor was also there, along with Elder Campbell. They both prayed for me before I was taken to surgery. I did struggle with this thought, as that day, December 16, was my son's birthday: *God, please don't let me die on my son's birthday* was my prayer. Then, I looked across the room and noticed that my oldest sister, Brenda, was crying, and Bruce's face had grown gloomy. With that, I melted into tears as I entered into the surgical room.

When I woke up, I learned that the surgery had been successful. I found my family still at attention. I admired their faithfulness to me.

My hospital stay was awful. During my surgery, my mouth had to be reconstructed. This made it difficult to eat as well as to take medicine. Apparently, no one had figured this out. The hospital staff gave me my meds whole. They served me a general diet. I am truly saddened by the ethics of some medical workers. The cleaners had more compassion than my medical team.

We were at the hospital on Christmas Day. I fought hard not to be overcome with depression; Bruce made this a team effort. Life had thoroughly changed for me. I was nowhere near being done with this ordeal. I also had to be fit for radiation in a few months. The medical staff wanted me to have a feeding tube. I flat out refused. *Enough of doing to me what you want. I will have some say-so about my care,* I thought. I must admit this decision was to my detriment. After ten days, I was discharged unable to eat, but that was my well-kept secret.

I felt so guilty lying to Bruce and others. I told everyone that I was eating when asked, knowing that I was unable to keep anything down, not even water, partially due to the reconstruction of my mouth. How I even remained alive assures me that there is a God.

After several weeks of weakness, it came time for radiation. I didn't know what to expect. Again, I had many informative agents. During this trial, I learned to do a lot of smiling and nodding. At the same time, I had the most ungodly thoughts about people.

The medical team conducting the radiation was awesome, quite different from the medical workers in my previous experiences. They were very concerned about my entire well-being. They were truly a godsend.

In spite of all their compassion, my first treatment was awful. The team placed a device over my head that reached to my shoulders, and they strapped me down. Then, once placed in the device, which I called a *furnace*, I yelled, "Let me out! I will just die! I want to leave! I'm tired!" Fearing I might have an aneurysm or a heart attack, they released me from the device.

CHAPTER 3

FAITH IN THE FURNACE

> When you walk through the fire you will not be
> burned. The fire will not set you ablaze. For I am
> with you.
>
> —Isaiah 43:2

Leaving the hospital without radiation treatment made me emotional. I felt defeated because this disease was robbing me of my very existence—embarrassed because I was out of control. All of this combined as what is defined as an anxiety attack. According to the medical staff, this reaction was normal. I therefore was prescribed a narcotic.

I received the narcotic with the objective of its sustaining me through my treatment. The device I was being placed in for radiation was very constrictive, and my claustrophobic nature was causing me anxiety attacks. I had no other choice; I had to take this narcotic.

My protest at taking this medicine was useless. It appeared as if I were losing control of making choices for my life, which caused me to become resentful. With each dose of medication, I lost my true existence. I was no longer able to study scripture. On the other hand, the medication was helping me maintain my stamina and got me through ten days of radiation.

On the eleventh day, I said, "Enough. If God is God, surely He could be my peace. After all, isn't He the prince of peace?" I remember studying, "As well as mine is stayed on thee, I'll keep in perfect peace" (Isaiah 26:3). I was to be anxious for nothing but make a prayer to God, and He would give me a peace which passeth all understanding (Philippians 4:6–7).

Surely, that was the outcome, and the medical staff could not believe that I was not taking my anxiety meds. I was experiencing such calmness without them. Again, I attribute this to the prayers that were made on my behalf.

Bruce continually prayed over me every morning. This strengthened me for my daily task. For a while, I didn't take notice of Bruce's needs. I admired him; he was so strong. He had placed aside his own challenges to be attentive toward me.

Nevertheless, I felt the need to rest him up. I suggested that we allow my sisters to participate in my commute to radiation. I was grateful that he agreed. The last thing I wanted was for him to suffer from burnout. Also, this would give me time with my sisters. I needed some feminine fellowship.

As each week went by, my radiation became more intense. Its impact on my body and mental state was great. I suffered severe weight loss and discoloration. I was dissipating right before my eyes. The mirror had become my greatest enemy. In my opinion, I looked like a dead man walking! This gave me the awful memory of my brothers dying, which made me feel like giving up. I would ask Bruce how he could stand to look at me. He simply responded, "Beauty is in the eye of the beholder." I told him love is blind.

On day fifteen, I called it quits again; I wished to be dead. I had the most compassionate staff working with me. My physician took special time to confer with me. He encouraged me so, telling me that I was halfway there—that I must reach the finish line.

I didn't have any tears to cry. The radiation had burned my tear ducts. I continued to cry from deep within. With what little strength I had, I reached for my Bible. It fell open to the page that documented the tale of the woman who had infirmity for twelve years. That story came alive to me. It encouraged me to get through the next five days. If she could endure twelve years, surely, I could endure thirty-two days.

It was easier said than done. Each day, I quoted the scripture, "Though I walk through the valley of the shadow of death I will fear no evil" (Psalm 23:4). That word had become my strength. I could feel the presence of God before me and behind me.

By day twenty-three, I endeavored to take one day at a time, as Matthew 6:25 instructs us to. Then one day, sitting at the foot of my bed, I glanced in the mirror. I didn't even recognize myself. All I could envision was my dad and oldest brother. I began to weep uncontrollably. Just then, my brother Michael called, giving me a prophetic word, warning me not to look in the mirror. I told him it was too late. Nevertheless, he continued with a word from God: looking in the mirror would weaken my faith. He reminded me that we walk by faith and not by sight. I struggled with walking by faith. It was as if I couldn't hold on anymore. I imagine most cancer patients are overcome with battle fatigue at some point. They simply just give up.

Against my brother's warning, I looked in the mirror one weekend. As I was facing the last five days of radiation, I looked in the mirror and told myself I would not return to radiation. In fact, I didn't want to even step outside anymore. All of a sudden, the darkness in the dungeon laid hold of me. It was as if the dungeon had arms. I fell to the floor, overcome by voices tormenting me with accusations of why I had contracted cancer. I was reminded of when, as a little girl, I used to rehearse the familiar Snow White quote "Mirror, mirror on the wall." The voices accused me of vanity, one of the sins God hates (Proverbs 6:17–19), and informed me that was the reason I had cancer.

The voices were indescribable and demonic. I felt as if I were being pulled into Hell. I began to cry out to God, saying, "I am sorry. I was just a kid. I didn't mean any harm. Please forgive me, Lord." I began to sob uncontrollably. I just knew my time on earth had come to an end!

Then, I heard what seemed like my mother's voice singing from outside my window, "When you see me crying, that's my train for your home."

Without a doubt, I knew I had left earth. There was no doubt in my mind I had died.

Just then, I experienced the warmest sensation all over my body, different from the heat I felt in radiation. It was soothing and speaking, saying, "Who do men say that I am? More importantly, who do you say that I am?" I remembered reading that somewhere. Yet I could not remember where. Before I knew it, my mouth was open: "I said you are the son of the living God!" I still wondered whether I were in heaven because then, the room shook as the voice said, "Upon this rock, I will build my church, and the gates of Hell shall not prevail. You are that rock, Lolita." (I never shared that with anyone; I did not want them to think I was delusional and in need of more medication.)

Most definitely, I had an encounter with Almighty God. What did that mean, and what was I to do? He definitely was a very present help in my time of trouble (Psalm 46:1).

I hoped that encounter would get me through the next five days. My mother's voice was very strengthening, just like her. She was very strong. To think she had made her way from heaven to encourage me. I had to make it. I thought, *All of heaven is rooting for me, as well as my family and friends down here on earth.*

Finally, the last day of radiation was here, along with the first day of the COVID-19 pandemic. That was quite ironic to me. This was meant to be a day of celebration. I didn't feel worthy to be celebrated. All my family was with me; my twin sisters, Laura and Carol, were present, along with my nieces and nephews. My pastor, Reverend Pitts, was there, along with Elder Campbell. They cheered as I entered the room to ring the bell. The bell-ringing ceremony was to indicate that I had successfully completed radiation!

I did not have the strength to ring the bell alone. A technician assisted me greatly. As the bell rang, it was as if the ceiling opened up to the heavens, with angels celebrating my endurance!

CHAPTER 4

THIS GIRL IS ON FIRE!

I have chosen you in the furnace of affliction refining

you as silver in the fire.

—Isaiah 48:10

My first day not having to go to radiation was disappointing. You would think I would have been rejoicing at the fact that my tormenting experience was over. The end of radiation marked the beginning of my recovery. But everything was a blur; my soul was in and out of time. What I mean by that is my world had drastically changed. The COVID-19 pandemic did not help me adapt. Why was all this happening at the same time? Now, among other things, I had to be concerned about contracting another terminal disease. I had to make a decision regarding quarantining and the day care center. This decision would affect my livelihood and create more stress, which I could not afford during my time of recovery. Decisions also had to be made about the nation's rehabilitation. The media had plagued the nation with fear!

Fear was a battle I had been fighting all through my diagnosis. I was not going to allow myself to be tormented by a disease I didn't have. After, by God's grace, I had overcome the disease that I did have, my weakness continued, as did my facade of eating. I felt so guilty saying I was eating when I wasn't. This guilt caused me to do some self-reflecting and soul-searching, which I believe is good for every soul. I began to reconsider my words and review my trial.

Is it really over? I wondered. *Will I return to who I was before? Right now, I am skin and bones. I have no hair.* Yet Bruce encouraged me, pointing out my inner beauty.

I spent several weeks low on energy. Opening my eyes was a challenge. Though the dungeon of darkness no longer had hold of me, it would still shout at me in my mind to despair. Every day, it was a challenge to make it through without crying and feeling sorry for myself. *What now?* was my question to God and myself. Everyone was telling me I would come out of this stronger. *How can I maximize on this adversity?* I thought. *How can I make what the enemy intended for evil turn out for my good?*

Three months prior to my diagnosis, I had considered visiting cancer centers. My ordeal had delayed my desire to do so. I shared my idea with no one. I didn't want to open myself up to naysayers. The pandemic paralyzed my pursuit of this endeavor. I had very little to busy myself with, other than writing this book, which was a road to my recovery. I was not going to allow myself to be stagnant. I had been on pause long enough. I continued to see God for my next endeavor. There was no way I could experience life as I had before. I viewed the world differently now.

Especially with everything slowing down from the pandemic, were the world and all its inhabitants moving independently of God? It seemed as if the world had been diagnosed with cancer as well. Was the world in need of radiation? Was all the world capable of handling a purification? I wanted to be an instrument of healing to the world around me and those in need. I had a burning desire to sit and pray with others. I had a testimony that I wanted to share. The testimony was "Be careful what you make a priority."

In life, I had always focused on weight control. I had certainly lost a lot of weight during my cancer treatment. Now, following my cancer treatment, I learned to be content with the image I had. I also discovered that to believe God through something is more challenging than to believe Him for something. To believe Him for healing you is one thing. However, to believe Him while sores cover your body is another.

This made me recall the servant Job as he picked the sores off his body (Job 7:5–7). Another thing Job suffered was the judgment of his friends. Again, well-meaning people insisted on telling me why I was afflicted with cancer. I had learned to bear the fruit of the spirit of temperance. Therefore, I nodded and smiled a lot.

I still wonder why those people felt as if God wouldn't speak to me concerning me. However, this made me seek God more. Therefore, in the stillness of my soul, I put questions before the Lord. They were answered by studying scripture, such as "You will find me when you seek me with all your heart" (Jeremiah 29:13).

I took a forty-year journey in forty days. In my soul-searching, I went back to when I was thirteen years old. Then, I was safe in my family's care; I talked as a child and thought as a child (1 Corinthians 13:11). Becoming older didn't make me stop my childlike thinking. I believe being the youngest of eight siblings delayed some of my maturity. I took life for granted. Losing loved ones allowed me to mature some.

I went to church on Sunday and performed good deeds throughout the week. Yet God wanted more, so as I did prior to my illness, I prayed to God about visiting cancer centers to help small children who were stricken with cancer. Did God have to place cancer in my body for me to be effective? I would have thought not. However, He did have to purify my heart. You see, the heart is deceitful and desperately wicked; who can know it? (Jeremiah 17:9). Somehow, I had deceived myself into thinking I was angelic and untouchable. Therefore, I would be applauded for serving in the cancer centers. We don't dare think our thoughts are as tainted as they are. That is the purpose of our works' being tried in the fire on judgment day (1 Corinthians 3:13).

However, on this journey, my motives were revealed. So was God chastising me? Maybe I was not exempt from chastising because as many as He loves, He chastises (Hebrews 12:6–7). I tend to think He was purifying me. You see, during my time of radiation, transformation took place. Impurities were eradicated not just from my body but from my soul as well. I no longer felt the importance placed on beauty and imagery. I was in the fight for my life. What was my real priority—keeping up an image of external beauty or finding inner peace? That is when I was aware though my outward man perished, my inner man was becoming renewed (2 Corinthians 4:6).

Certainly, God had given me beauty for ashes. Well, reading the scriptures, I found that almost worth the journey. To be chosen by God for refinement was humbling. I had attended church all my life. Now, I was having one-on-one conversations with Him. I mean, He did not speak to me as He did Moses. Yet I felt a burning in my heart every time I met with Him (Luke 24:32). I now was experiencing the fullness of joy in the presence of the Lord (Psalm 16:11).

"How can you experience joy?" was the question of many. When during my recovery I had to be pushed around in a wheelchair, people found it hard to look at me. I saw the sadness in their eyes. However, I had a bigger vision than the eyes could see. You see, their eyes had not seen nor had their ears heard what God had in store for me.

I know I have quoted several scriptures, but this is the flyer I'm speaking of. As a child, I was baptized in water. As an adult, I have now been baptized in fire—"this girl is on fire." Medical science eradicated my cancer with radiation. God gave me a new way of thinking via illumination. As Jesus and the children of Israel were late in the wilderness, so was I. In the wilderness, I was humbled. I have no problem admitting I needed to be humbled. It's impossible to be used by God without being humbled. Whosoever shall exalt himself shall be humbled. Whosoever humbles himself shall be exalted. Yes, I didn't think I deserved cancer, but who does? If God would mark sin, who would stand? (Psalm 130:3). I really tried to get through this chapter without so much scripture. But reading this was like fire shooting up into my bones; I would learn to say nothing lest I heard my Father say it (John 8:28).

Many things I've learned during my time of recovery, one being man shall not live by bread alone. This was proven during my time of radiation, when I went over forty days without eating or drinking. I wondered whether God had orchestrated this. I was so weak during my treatment, I had nothing but Him to sustain me. Had He forced me to fast? I wouldn't have done it otherwise, and fat doctors wouldn't have allowed it.

So I gathered that during my time of radiation, God had been transforming me. I looked nothing like I had before. I had been with God the whole time and had not been aware.

One night, a man dreamed he was walking along a beach with the Lord when across the sky flashed scenes of his life. He noticed two sets of footprints in the sand, one belonging to him and the other to the Lord. When the last scene flashed, only one set of footprints in the sand remained. Also, he noticed the second set of footprints disappeared at the lowest and saddest parts of his life. This really bothered him, and he questioned the Lord about it. "Lord, You said once I decided to follow You, You'd walk with me all the way. But I noticed during the troublesome times in my life, there was only one set of footprints. I don't understand; when I needed You the most, why did You leave me?" The Lord replied, "I love you and never would leave you. During your trials and suffering, when you saw only one set of footprints, it was then I carried you."

You see, scripture says that this light affliction cannot be compared to the glory that shall be revealed in you. It's true, dear reader, no doubt I experienced hell on earth with cancer. I can't describe to you my downtrodden mental state. I simply then made a feeble attempt to encourage others afflicted with such, as well as their family members. Silence speaks volumes, and "Be slow to speak" is my advice to those who are giving care to cancer victims. Cancer victims, call on Him, and He will answer you and show you great and mighty things (Jeremiah 29:13).

As I write this book, I am deep in sorrow. My eyes are unable to form tears. Yet I grieve for the cancer patients experiencing what I have experienced. Not everyone has the family support that I had. Perhaps they don't have the financial access that I had either. More importantly, they might not have the knowledge of my Lord and Savior. Whatever the case, I am praying for them. While I have breath in my body, I will daily lift up a prayer for cancer victims and their families.

If the Lord says so and grants me grace, I will spend a great portion of my life giving back. For this cause, I was called into the kingdom. (All work that was done prior to this I consider filth that I may gain the Excellency of Christ; Philippians 3:8.)

I will shake everything that can be shaken, and that which remains, shall remain. For I am a Consuming Fire (Hebrews 12:27–29 KJV).